This revision guide i
the OCR GCSE specification.
The aim is to provide you with
summary notes and key terms on
all of the topics.
Specification links are given in
the contents

Contents

Chapter 1 Introduction to Economics

Definitions

The Basic Economic Problem - there are limited resources but wants are infinite, this means that choices have to be made.

Scarce resources - those which are not unlimited in supply e.g. oil.

Non- renewable resources - resources which will eventually run out e.g. oil and coal.

Renewable resources - resources which can regenerate e.g. wind and solar energy.

Free good - a good which does not cost anything e.g. air and sea water NB free samples are not free goods because they cost the supplier.

Economic good - a good which has a cost e.g. coffee and biscuits.

A positive economic statement - objective statements which can be tested e.g. a reduction in the price of ice cream will increase the demand.

A normative statement - an opinion / value judgement e.g. more should be spent on the NHS.

Ceteris Paribus - 'all other things are equal'. When testing economic theory we only change one thing at a time to assess the impact of that change.

Opportunity cost - the benefit of the next best alternative forgone e.g. if the government spends more on schools they have less to spend on the NHS.

Economic sustainability - the best use of resources to create responsible development or growth, now and in the future

Social sustainability - the impact of development or growth that promotes an improvement in the quality of life now and in the future

Environmental sustainability - where there is a small impact on the environment now and in the future due to development or growth

Market - a place where buyers and sellers meet to exchange goods and services

Market economy - resources are allocated by supply and demand

Specialisation - where an individual, firm, region or economy focuses production on one good or narrow range of goods e.g. Apple specialises in technology; the UK specialises in financial services.

Division of labour - a type of specialisation where a worker focuses on one task e.g. on a car production line or a teacher specialising in teaching economics.

The Key Economic Decisions
What to produce? How to produce? and for whom to produce?

Factors of Production
Land - this is the space as well as the natural resources in it and on it. E.g. minerals, sea water, car park, area where the firm is built.

Labour - the workers e.g. chefs, cleaners.
Quality of workers i.e. skills is important as well as the quantity. A country with a large unskilled labour force will have lower growth.

Capital - man made resources such as machinery, factories and equipment used to produce goods and services.
Spending more on capital goods will help a business grow.

Enterprise - the factor which brings together the other factors of production and takes risks in order to make a profit.

Rewards to the factors of production
Land - rent
Labour - wages
Capital - interest
Enterprise - profit

Economic Agents

Producers - firms which produce goods and services.
Goals - maximise profit; maximise sales; maximise revenue; ethical objectives.

Consumers - people who buy the goods and services.
Goals - maximise utility/ satisfaction, maximise wages.

Government - set the rules and produce some goods and services.
Goals - maximise welfare of the citizens; economic growth; low inflation; full employment; equilibrium in the balance of payments.

Costs and Benefits of Economic Choices

Economic Sustainability
Benefits include

- Increased sales

- Increased profits

- More innovative products

Costs include

- Costs of production

- Price the consumers pay

Social Sustainability

- A happier society may lead to increased productivity over time.
- Encourages fairness

Environmental Sustainability

- Use of renewable resources can mean a continued use of raw materials
- Use of non-renewable resources makes production more difficult in the future
- Air pollution can lead to breathing problems

Examples of Markets
Shop
Auction
eBay
An actual market (with stall holders, held outside)
Online shopping
Catalogues

Sectors of the Economy
Primary - extraction of raw materials e.g. fishing, oil, agriculture
Secondary - manufacturing raw materials into final goods e.g. building hotels, making clothes
Tertiary - service sector e.g. selling of goods, tourism, health care, transport

Factor and Product Markets
Factor market is where the services of factors of production are bought and sold for example households supply labour to firms or a farmer may rent land of a household to keep animals.
Goods/product market is where the final goods and services are sold e.g. shops and online

Advantages of Specialisation
- Firms/countries can focus on what they are best at or have the resources for.

- Higher quality and better products can be produced.

- Larger output due to focusing on a narrow range of goods - larger economies of scale so lower average costs.

- A reputation can be established.

Disadvantages of Specialisation
- Countries will not be self-sufficient; a problem in times of war or trade disputes.

- A country may rely on raw materials which eventually run out.

- Transport costs may mean that there are no/ minimal benefits from trading.

Advantages of Division of Labour

- Workers can focus on the task they are best at so efficiency is improved.

- Workers may be more motivated as they are doing the job they enjoy/are best at.

- Less equipment will be needed if the worker is only doing one task.

- Less training required if the worker is only focusing on one task/small range of tasks.

Disadvantages of Division of Labour

- Workers may become bored/demotivated and make mistakes if they are working on a menial task on a production line.

- If one worker on a production line is slow/unwell all the stages after that worker get slowed down.

- Workers find it hard to get another job as they have a narrow range of skills.

Chapter 2   Demand and Supply

Definitions

Demand - the quantity consumers are willing and able to buy at a given price.

Individual demand - demand for a product by an individual person

Market demand - demand for the product from all individuals added together.

Supply - the quantity that suppliers are willing and able to supply at a given price.

Individual supply - the supply by one individual firm

Market supply - the supply of a product by all firms added together.

Normal goods - as income increases demand increases e.g. clothes.

Inferior goods - as income increases demand decreases e.g. spam, public transport

Joint demand/ complements - goods which are consumed together e.g. tea and biscuits.

Competitive demand/ substitutes - goods which are alternatives e.g. bounty and twix.

Derived demand - the demand for a good is due to the demand for another good e.g. the demand for wood is derived due to the demand for tables.

Price elasticity of demand (PED) - the responsiveness of quantity demanded due to a change in price.
PED = % change in quantity demanded / % change in price

Price elasticity of supply (PES) - the responsiveness of quantity supplied due to a change in price.

PES = % change in quantity supplied / % change in price

The Demand Curve

A reduction in price leads to an increase in demand known as an extension in demand.

An increase in price leads to a decrease in demand known as a contraction in demand.

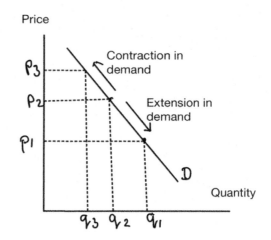

Shifts in the Demand Curve to the Right

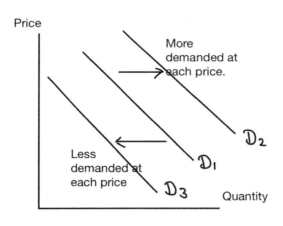

- An increase in income if the good is a normal good e.g. takeaways

- A decrease in income for an inferior good e.g. spam

- An increase in population/ an increase in the number of people in a certain age group e.g. an ageing population will mean more demand for bungalows.

- An increase in the price of a substitute e.g. if the price of bounty goes up the demand for twix will increase

- A decrease in the price of a complement e.g. if the price of strawberries falls the demand for cream will increase

- Changes in tastes and preferences e.g. advertising of the good or popularity of the good changes such as ice creams in the summer.

The Supply Curve

An increase in price means suppliers are prepared to supply more due to the higher profit margin. There will be an extension in supply

A decrease in price will lead to a contraction in supply.

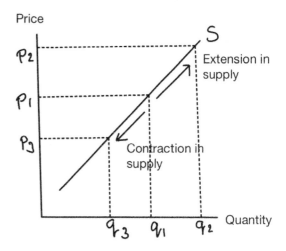

Shifts in the Supply Curve to the right

Lowering the costs of production will means suppliers are prepared to supply more at each price due to the higher profit.

- Lower price of raw materials

- Lower energy costs

- Improvements in technology

- Lower labour costs e.g. labour becomes more productive so cost per unit of output is lower

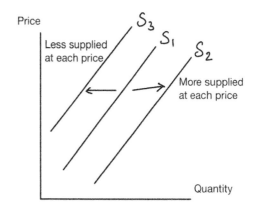

- Subsidies (taxes will shift supply to the left)

Equilibrium Price

When price is P2 there will be excess supply of q3-q2. The price will fall to Pe to sell the excess supply.

When price is P3 there will be excess demand of q3-q2. The price will increase to Pe to ration out the shortage.

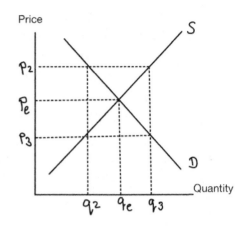

Changes in Equilibrium Price

E.g. There is an increase in income
The demand curve for iPhones will shift to the right because they are a normal good. This will lead to an increase in price from P1 to P2 and an increase in quantity traded from q1 to q2. There will be an extension in supply

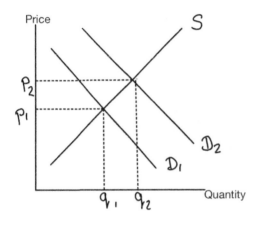

Eg The government gives a subsidy to farmers producing milk.

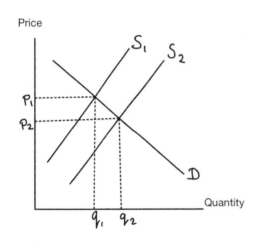

The supply curve for milk will shift to the right. There will be an extension in demand. Price falls from P1 to P2, quantity traded increases from q1 to q2.

E.g. An increase in cost of cocoa and government campaigns to encourage people to eat healthier. The demand curve for chocolate will shift left due to change in tastes and preference. The supply curve will shift left due to increase in costs of production.
Price increase from P1 to P2, quantity traded falls from q1 to q2.

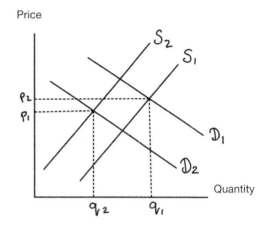

Price Elasticity of Demand

Types of Elasticity

When price increases demand falls so PED will always be negative. When determining the type of elasticity the numerical value is considered, the negative sign is ignored eg if PED is -5 the goodwill have elastic demand because 5 is greater than 1.

Inelastic demand PED < 1

When price is P1 total revenue = A + B
When price is P2 total revenue = A + C
Area C is bigger than area B so when price increases TR increases for goods with inelastic demand.

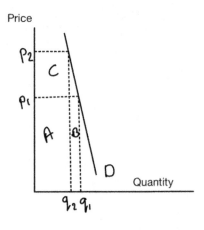

Elastic demand PED > 1
When price is P1 total revenue = A + B
When price is P2 total revenue = A + C
Area C is smaller than area B so when price increases TR decreases for goods with inelastic demand.

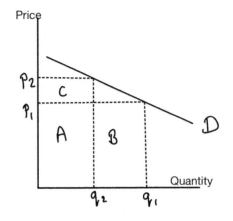

Unitary elastic demand PED = 1
When price is P1 total revenue = A + B
When price is P2 total revenue = A + C
Area B = Area C so TR stays the same
when price increases

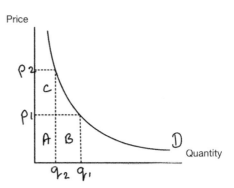

Extreme elasticities
Perfectly inelastic demand
PED = 0

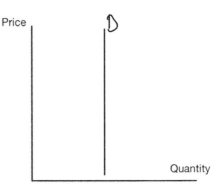

Perfectly elastic demand
PED = infinity

Factors Determining PED

- Number of substitutes - if there are many substitutes a rise in price will mean consumers have alternatives to chose from so there will be a big reduction in demand ie demand will be elastic eg chocolate buttons.

- Proportion of income spent on the good - if the good takes up a large proportion of a consumers income an increase in price will be significant so there will be a big reduction in demand ie demand will be elastic eg holidays.

- Luxury or necessity - if the good is a necessity a rise in price will not have much impact on demand for the good ie demand will be inelastic eg toilet rolls

- Addiction - if the consumer is addicted a rise in price will have little impact on demand ie demand will be inelastic eg cigarettes.

- Brand loyalty - if consumers are loyal to a brand, when price increases they will not cut consumption by much ie demand will be inelastic eg Apple iPhone.

- Time - in the short run consumers may not be able to switch to an alternative as it takes time to find a suitable substitute. In the short run demand will often be inelastic but in the long run more elastic.

Price Elasticity of Supply

PES will always be positive - as price increases, suppliers wish to supply more

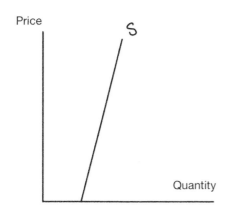

Inelastic supply
PES < 1

Hard to increase supply when price increases

Elastic supply
PES > 1

Easy to increase supply when price increases

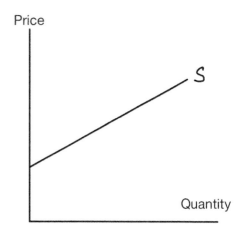

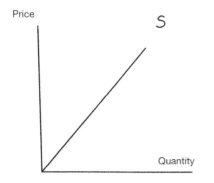

Unitary elastic supply
PES = 1

Perfectly inelastic supply
PES = 0

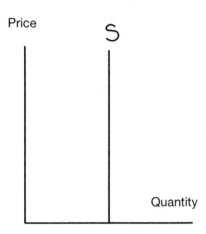

Perfectly elastic supply
PES = infinity

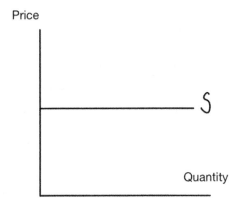

Factors Determining PES

1. Stock levels - if the firm has high levels of the product in storage it is easy to increase supply in response to a rise in price. Supply will be elastic. This tends to be the case with non-perishable goods or goods which do not go out of fashion e.g. shampoo.

2. Level of unemployment - when unemployment is high it is easy to increase supply as it is easy to get more workers to produce more. Supply will be elastic.

3. Time to grow/ produce - goods which take a long time to grow will have inelastic supply as supply cannot be increased quickly e.g. apples.

4. Time period - in short run it may be hard for a firm to increase supply due to factors of production being fixed. Supply will be more inelastic in the short run. In the long run more machinery can be bought or they can move to a bigger factory.

Chapter 3 Competition and Production

Definitions

Competitive markets - many buyers and sellers

Oligopoly - a few large firms e.g. supermarkets

Monopoly - one large firm dominates the market

Production - total output

Productivity - output per unit of input

Fixed costs - costs which do not increase when output increases e.g. rent.

Variable costs - costs which increase when output increases e.g. ingredients.

Total cost = fixed costs + variable costs.

Average cost = total cost / quantity.

Total Revenue/ Turnover = Price x Quantity

Average Revenue = Total Revenue / Price.

Profit = Total revenue - Total cost.
Economies of Scale - lower average costs for a firm when they increase their scale of production.

Internal economies of scale - cost advantages with the firm

External economies of scale - cost advantages due to the firm being part of a growing industry.

Diseconomies of scale - increased average costs when the first gets too big.

Why do Producers Compete?
- To increase profit
- To enter a new market
- To survive in a market
- To force competitors out of a market

How do Producers Compete?
Price competition - lowering the price in order to encourage more consumers to buy the product and move away from competitors
Non-price competition- persuading customers to buy the product by improving quality, offering loyalty cards, offering better customer service.

Increased competition in the market will shift supply curve to the right leading to a fall in price.

Impact of Competition

Producers
- May need to cut costs in order to maintain profits

- Need to innovate to ensure quality is the best

- Need to improve productivity to lower production costs

- May lose customers to competitors and go out of business

- May need to seek to replace workers with machines to reduce costs

Consumers
- Lower prices so higher living standards

- Improved quality

- More choice

- Innovations might be negative e.g. lower fat foods have other harmful chemicals

- Quality may fall if producers are looking to reduce costs

- Increased advertising to persuade consumers to buy the product may mean consumers buy things they do not really want

Monopoly
- One large firm

- Legal monopoly is 25% or more market share

- Price makers

- Tends to be high prices

- Tend not to be efficient as due to lack of competition they do not need to be

- May be efficient if they benefit from economies of scale

- Large profits so may be efficient if they invest

- Hard for new firms to join the market

Oligopoly
- A few large firms dominate the market

- Price makers but need similar prices to competitors

- Price and quality depends on competitors but tend to be lower than monopoly and higher than competitive

- Generally, not very efficient but more efficient than monopoly due to the competition in the market

Competitive Market
- A large number of small firms

- Price takers - price set by the market

- Price tends to be lower due to high amounts of competition

- Tend to be efficient

The Role of Producers
- Usually aim to make profit

- Employ workers

- Producers may be self-employed e.g. driving instructors

- Producers may be firms e.g. Tesco

- Government is producer of police, education, health care

Production
Advantages of an increase in production
- Reduced unemployment

- More goods for consumers to buy so increased standard of living

- Increase profit

- More scope for economies of scale so lower average cost

- Economic growth for the country

Disadvantages of an increase in production
- The increased profits may be used to buy machines to replace workers

- If the output increases too much there may be diseconomies of scale so higher average costs

- Increased production, if not green, will harm the environment

Productivity
How is Productivity increased ?
- Specialisation of the workers

- Training of the workers

- More technology to make production more efficient

- Increased benefits to workers to increase motivation

Advantages of Increased Productivity
- Lower average costs for firms so they can lower prices and be more internationally competitive

- More exports

- Possibly increased employment if there is more demand for exports

- Increased profits which can be re invested

- Increased total output for an economy

Disadvantages of Increased Productivity
- May lead to unemployment if workers replaced by machines or if fewer workers now needed

- If more goods are exported, other countries may impose tariffs to make the goods more expensive

Economies of Scale

Internal Economies of Scale

- Purchasing economies - larger firms can buy raw materials in bulk and negotiate discounts which will lower the cost per unit.

- Financial economies - larger firms will be less of a risk to banks so likely get a lower interest rate on loans.

- Risk-bearing economies - larger firms can diversify into different markets or different countries to spread risks. If one product is doing badly another would hopefully be doing well. E.g. supermarkets used to just sell food now they have phone shops, currency and pharmacies.

- Marketing economies - larger firms have a bigger marketing budget so can advertise at football matches for example. A larger firm can advertise several products as part of the brand at the same time. This means the per unit advertising cost is lower.

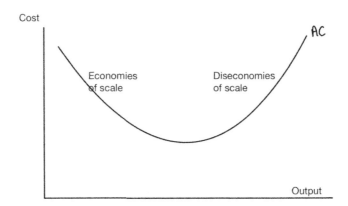

- Managerial economies - as the firm grows the number of managers does not grow so the managerial cost per unit falls. Larger firms can afford to employ specialists who will be more qualified/ more efficient.

- Technical economies - larger firms can spend on specialist equipment which is faster and lowers unit cost. A bigger lorry which can deliver 4 times as much is not going to cost 4 times as much and will still only require one driver so the unit costs of delivery will fall.

External Economies of Scale

- Many firms in one location can share resources such as waste disposal.

- Suppliers of raw materials may locate nearby.

- Local training courses may locate nearby so there will be a large pool of skilled workers.

- There may be a better transport network making deliveries easier as well as easier for workers to get to work.

- Shared research and development facilities.

Diseconomies of Scale

- Communication problems - harder to communicate when there are more people, workers might not be clear about what they should be doing.

- Managers will have less control as the firm grows.

- More wastage as materials may get lost in a bigger warehouse.

- Co-ordination problems - might be harder to co-ordinate between departments.

- Lower motivation - workers may feel less valued so lower productivity

Chapter 4 The Labour Market

Definitions
Demand for labour - firms demand for workers

Supply of labour - workers offering themselves for work

Gross pay - amount paid before deductions

Net pay - amount paid after deductions

Deductions - income tax, national insurance and pension

Income tax - a percentage tax on income

National Insurance - a tax paid by workers and their employer on income

Occupational mobility - workers can easily move between jobs with different skills

Geographical mobility - workers can easily move between different parts of the country

Reasons for Immobility of Labour
- Workers have the wrong skills

- Workers do not want to relocate

- Workers are not aware of jobs in other areas

- Workers are tied to an area e.g. due to family or owning a house

Wage Rate Determination

Wages are determined by the supply and demand for labour.

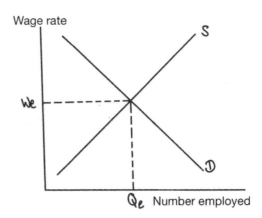

Factors Shifting Demand Curve for Labour

- Demand for the product - if demand for the product increases more workers will be needed

- Productivity of labour - if workers are more productive firms will want to employ more workers (rather than use machines)

- Profits of the firm - higher profits mean the firm can expand and take on more workers

- Price of the product - if the product increases in price each worker generates more revenue for the firm so demand for labour will increase

- State of the economy - if the economy is growing more workers will be needed to produce more goods

Factors Shifting the Supply Curve for Labour

- Benefits from work - if benefits such as private health care or flexible hours increases then more workers will want to work so supply shifts right

- Other monetary payments - if bonuses or performance related pay increases more workers will want to work so supply shifts right

- Education and training - more workers will be able to work if they have more skills

- Barriers to entry - if fewer skills are needed for a job there will be increased supply of labour to that job

- Size of the working population - increased retirement age, fall in school leaving age, increased immigration will increase the size of the labour force

Chapter 5 The Role of Money and Financial Markets

Definitions
Money - anything which can be used in exchange for goods and services

Barter - exchanging goods for other goods

Commercial Banks - banks which individuals and firms use - high street banks e.g. TSB, NatWest

Investment banks - banks for firms with specialist needs such as issuing shares e.g. Goldman Sachs

Building Society - mutual organisations owned by their members e.g. Nationwide

Insurance companies - individuals or firms are given financial protection from an event e.g. pet insurance will pay out if your pet gets sick.

Saving - part of income which is not spent

Investment - purchase of capital goods by firms

The Role of Money
Examples of money - bank notes, coins, savings account, current account

Money is a medium of exchange so allows people to buy goods and services

The Role of the Financial Sector
- Consumers, firms and government can purchase goods and services
- Consumers, firms and government can borrow money
- Money which people save is used to lend to those who need to borrow

The Role of Banks

Central Banks e.g. Bank of England
- Issue notes and coins

- Control interest rates (monetary policy)

- Manages a countries foreign exchange reserves

- Acts as a bank for commercial banks

- Acts as bank for the government

- Provides financial stability

Commercial Banks eg NatWest
- Accept deposits from customers

- Accept cheques from customers

- Issue loans

- Provide foreign currency

- Offer safe deposit boxes

- Make payments for customers via card, phone, bank transfer

Investment Banks
- Assist firms with mergers and takes overs

- Issue shares on behalf of firms

- Advise firms on raising finance e.g. for expansion

- Assist firms with international trade

Building Societies eg Nationwide
- Similar functions to banks but on a smaller scale

Insurance Companies

- Pay compensation to firm and individuals when events take place e.g. accidents

- Life insurance - pay out to the family if a person dies.

Importance of the Financial Sector
Consumers

- Can borrow money and pay later

- Can save money and earn interest

- Can spread risk by having insurance or having multiple bank accounts/shares

Producers

- Can borrow money to expand

- Can have short term overdrafts whilst waiting for payments to come in

- Can reduce risk of non-payment if they have insurance

Government

- Allows them to borrow in order to spend e.g. to get out of recession

- Allows them to borrow short term and long term

- Enables them to spend even if they don't know when the revenue will be coming in

Impact of Interest Rates
Savings

As interest rates increase people tend to want to save more as the return on savings will be higher.

Borrowing

As the rate of interest increases individual and firms are less likely to borrow as it will cost them more

Investment

Firms are more likely to invest when the rate of interest is lower because borrowing money to invest is cheaper

Chapter 6   Economic Objectives

Definitions

Economic growth - increase in the productive potential of an economy.

GDP - the value of output produced in a year.

GDP per capita - national income per person.
Real GDP - national income adjusted for inflation.

Recession - two successive quarters of negative economic growth.

Boom - when the economy is growing quickly.

The level of unemployment - number of people looking for a job who do not have a job.

The rate of unemployment - the number unemployed as a % of the labour force.

Claimant count - number of people claiming unemployment benefit related payments.

The Labour force survey (ILO) - uses a sample of the population to count those who are out of work and actively seeking work.

Full employment - where everyone of working age who wants to work has a job at the current wage rate.

Underemployment - when someone has a job but the job does not fully utilise their skills or when someone is working part time but wants to work full time.

Frictional unemployment - unemployment for a short period of time between jobs.

Seasonal unemployment - unemployment due to the season e.g. ski instructors will be unemployed in the summer.

Cyclical unemployment - unemployment due to the economy being in the recession stage of the economic cycle.

Structural unemployment - unemployment due to the change in structure of the economy e.g. coal mines closing down.

Distribution of income - how money is distributed between the population.
Income - a flow of money e.g. rent, wages, interest, profit, benefits.

Wealth - a stock at a point in time which includes the total of all assets e.g. house, business, cash, jewelry.

Inequality - uneven distribution, usually referring to income or wealth.

Inflation - a sustained rise in the average price level or fall in the value of money.

Deflation - a fall in average price level.

Disinflation - the rate or inflation is falling but prices are still rising.

Hyperinflation - very high inflation.

Macro Economic Objectives

Economic growth
Low unemployment
Fair distribution of income
Price stability

Economic Growth

Determinants of Economic Growth
An increase in the quantity and/or quality of the factors of production for example

- Better education and training for workers

- An increase in the size of the working population e.g. through immigration

- Investment in better/faster technology

- More technology

- Governments subsidies to encourage investment

- Discovery of new natural resources e.g. oil

Benefits of Economic Growth
- Wages are usually rising so higher standards of living.

- Higher wages so increased spending, more profit for firms.

- Higher wages, more income tax for government.

- More profit for firms leads to more investment.

- More profit for firms means more tax revenue.

- More demand for goods leads to more demand for labour so reduced unemployment.

- Firms have more money so may invest in greener technology.

- Greater tax revenue for the government and less need to spend on benefits so there may be a budget surplus which can be used to pay back national debt.

Costs of Economic Growth

- Inequality may increase as often the rich are getting richer.

- Finite resources get used up so may increase in price.

- Habitats are destroyed.

- Negative externalities due to increased production e.g. pollution and congestion

- Working hours may be longer.

- If supply cannot keep up with demand there will be demand pull inflation.

- Increased income means increased spending on imports worsening the balance of payments.

- If prices increase goods will become less internationally competitive

Economic, Social and Environmental Sustainability

- Economic growth ought to improve quality of life now without sacrificing growth for future generations.

- Rising seas levels reduce the amount of land available in the future

- Increased growth harms the environment for future generations

Unemployment

Problems of Unemployment

- Lower incomes, less spending power, lower standard of living

- Fewer goods and services produced, less profit for firms.

- Firms have less money for investment.

- The government will need to spend more on benefits.

- Increased levels of crime, depression and family break ups.

- Less tax revenue for the government from income tax, VAT and corporation tax.

- Regions can suffer if there are high levels of unemployment, local firms have fewer customers so less profit

Benefits of Unemployment

- Firms find it easier to recruit workers as there are more to choose from

- Workers may accept lower wages which keeps costs down for firms, firms will be more internationally competitive

- Less demand due to lower incomes will lead to lower inflation

Policies to Reduce Unemployment

- Reduce interest rates to increases demand for goods.

- Reduce taxation e.g. income tax so people have more money to spend.

- Education and training to improve occupational immobility.

- Subsidies to firms to encourage them to invest in areas of high unemployment.

- Lower minimum wage so firms can afford to employ more workers.

Fair Distribution of Income

Causes of Differences in Distribution of Income and Wealth
Income
- Individuals who have assets e.g. a business or a house to rent are able to earn income from the assets.

- Difference in wages which are due to many factors such as skills, education, minimum wage, responsibilities.

- Benefits - these tend to be lower than wages.

- Age - younger workers tend to earn less, older people are often living off a pension.

- Gender - often women get paid less than men as they take out time for children or are working part time.

Wealth
- Inheritance e.g. inheriting a house from parents.

- Savings - those who earn more are able to save more.

- Those with more money can buy property to live in or rent out.

- Business - those with ideas and / or money can start up a business which can be worth a lot.

Consequences of Differences in Distribution of Income and Wealth
Costs of Inequality
- Poverty

- Poor housing

- Poor health

- Poor education - in countries where education is not free

- Social problems

- Lower economic growth

Benefits of Inequality

- Creates incentives for people to work harder to earn more

- Tickle down - those with higher incomes set up businesses and employ other people generating more jobs

Price Stability

Measures of Inflation
Consumer Price Index (CPI)
This is the main measure used in the UK. The target rate of inflation in the UK is 2%. The price of a typical basket of goods is calculated. In the base year this is given the value 100. Inflation for the year is calculated by recalculating the price of the basket of goods. Items in the basket of goods is updated regularly to reflect trends e.g. hand gel was added recently.

Retail Price Index (RPI)
This tends to be higher than CPI as it includes mortgage interest payments and council tax.

Problems with CPI and RPI
- Only a sample of the population is used.

- Households may not record accurate information.

- The basket of goods is only updated once a year e.g. hand gel was added in 2021 when there had been a significant increase in demand during 2020.

Types of Inflation
Demand-pull inflation
Caused when supply cannot keep up with demand
Examples:
- increased income

- reduced income tax

- reduction in interest rates

- high consumer confidence

- increased demand for exports

Cost-push inflation
Caused by increased costs of production.
Examples:

- increased wages

- increased raw material prices

- imported raw material increase in price

- increased oil prices

- increased tax

Problems of Inflation

- Cost of living increases so consumers can buy fewer goods and services.

- Workers may ask for pay rises so cost of production increases leading to further inflation.

- Shoe leather costs - cost of searching for the best prices in a climate of rising prices.

- Menu costs - costs of updating prices lists.

- International competitiveness falls so fewer exports will be bought.

- Uncertainty may mean less consumption and less investment.

Deflation
Although rising prices are generally not good, falling prices are undesirable in some situations.

- If deflation is due to falling costs of production perhaps due to better technology this will not be a problem.

- If deflation is due to low aggregate demand, firms may have to reduce prices to get rid of stock. This is undesirable.

- Deflation generally means the economy is doing badly.

- Lower prices mean less profit for firms or possibly even loss if they are having to heavily discount old stock.

Usefulness of Inflation Figures

- Employers use the figures to determine pay rises - pay needs to keep up with inflation otherwise workers will see a fall in their real wage.

- Trade unions use the figures when bargaining for higher wages for their workers.

- Government uses the figures to establish how much to increase pensions and benefits.

Chapter 7   Government Policy

Definitions

Fiscal policy - using government spending and taxation to influence aggregate demand.

Tight/deflationary fiscal policy - reducing government spending and increasing taxation to reduce aggregate demand.

Expansionary/reflationary fiscal policy - increasing government spending and reducing taxation to increase aggregate demand.

Progressive tax - as income increases the % of income on this tax increases e.g. income tax in the UK.

Regressive tax - as income increases the % of income on this tax decreases e.g. car tax

Proportional tax - as income increases the % of income on this tax stays the same. E.g. VAT if everyone were to spend all of their income (unlikely).

Direct tax- tax on income e.g. income tax and corporation tax.

Indirect tax - tax on spending e.g. VAT and excise duty.

Budget deficit - government spending is greater than taxation in a year.

Budget surplus - government spending is less than taxation in a year.

Balanced budget - government spending and taxation are equal in a year.

National debt - accumulated budget deficits.

Monetary policy - manipulation of interest rates, the money supply and exchange rates to influence aggregate demand.

Tight/deflationary monetary policy - increasing interest rates to reduce aggregate demand.

Expansionary monetary policy - reducing interest rates to increase aggregate demand.

Supply-side policies - policies aimed at increasing the productive potential of an economy.

Fiscal Policy

The Impact of Fiscal Policy on the Macro Economic Objectives
Expansionary fiscal policy is often used in a recession. Increased government spending will increase aggregate demand because government spending is a component of AD.
Reduced income tax will increase consumption because consumers now have more money.
Reduced corporation tax will mean firms have more profit for investment.
Overall spending will increase so output increases, GDP increases, more workers are needed to produce the additional output meaning unemployment will reduce. The additional demand may lead to an increase in the price level.

Benefits of Fiscal Policy
- Expansionary fiscal policy can lead of economic growth and a reduction in unemployment
- Contractionary fiscal policy can reduce the rate of inflation
- Increasing progressive tax can lead to a more equal distribution of income

Costs of Fiscal Policy
- Expansionary can lead to an increase in debt for the government
- Expansionary may lead of an increase spending on imports rather than UK produced goods
- If the economy is in recession the reduction in tax may not increase spending due to low confidence.
- Increased income tax could lead to increased tax avoidance
- Increased income tax could lead to people / firms leaving the country
- Higher income tax means less incentive for people to work

Monetary Policy

Interest Rates

In the UK interest rates are set by the Monetary Policy Committee (MPC) of the Bank of England. They meet once a month to discuss whether interest rates should be changed. They have been given a target of 2% inflation.

How Interest Rates Impact Aggregate Demand

An Increase in interest rates will:

- Increase incentive to save due to higher returns which means less consumption.

- Make it more expensive to take out loans e.g. for a new car or house extension so less consumption.

- Increase interest payments on existing loans or mortgages (unless they are fixed rate) so less money to spend on other consumption.

- More expensive for firms to take out loans so less investment.

- Lower consumer and business confidence so less consumption and investment.

- Higher demand for saving money in UK banks so increased demand for pounds. This will increase the exchange rate. Exports become more expensive so fall in exports. Imports become cheaper so rise in Imports.

All of the above lead to a reduction in aggregate demand. This is known as tight monetary policy.

Impact on the Macroeconomic Objectives

A reduction in demand will lead to lower economic growth and increased unemployment (due to fewer workers needed). There will be downward pressure on prices.

Problems with Monetary Policy

- There is a time lag of approximately 2 years before the full effect is experienced.

- It is difficult to get accurate data on how much interest rates need changing by.

- The impact depends on the size of the change in interest rates

- Lower interest rates may not increase consumption if confidence is low.

Supply-side Policies

Examples of Supply-side Policies and their impact on Objectives

- Reduce unemployment benefits - this will encourage more people to take a job, more people- working increases the potential output. This will reduce unemployment

- Reduce income tax - this increases incentives for people who were not working to work as they now take home more of their earnings. This will reduce unemployment

- Improve labour market flexibility - making it easier for firms to make workers redundant when they are not needed means firms will be more willing to take on workers short term. This will reduce unemployment and can also increase economic growth

- Reduce power of trade unions - less time lost through strikes. Increasing economic growth due to more output

- Improve education and training - workers have more skills and will be more productive. Increase economic growth.

- Incentives for firms to invest e.g. tax breaks - more investment e.g. in technology will increase productive capacity. This will increase economic growth and may reduce price level

- Trade liberalisation - removing barriers to trade between countries means goods and capital can be traded more freely. Improve balance of payment and reduce inflation. May increase economic growth if exports increase

- Privatisation - selling state owned assets and splitting them into parts increases competition encouraging firms to be more productive. This increases economic growth and may reduce inflation

- Deregulation - removing rules can increase competition and improve efficiency. Increase economic growth and reduce inflation

Problems with Supply-side Policies

- There is usually a long time lag for them to fully take effect e.g. education can take many years.

- Some policies are politically unacceptable e.g. reducing unemployment benefit.

- Labour market reforms means workers have less job security.

- Some policies lead to increased inequality e.g. cutting benefits.

- They may be costly to implement so will have an opportunity cost to the government.

Chapter 8 Limitations of Markets

Definitions

Positive externality/external benefit - benefit to a 3rd party e.g. when someone has flowers in their garden other people can enjoy them.

Negative externality/external cost - cost to a 3rd party e.g. noise from building works

Indirect tax - tax on goods and services e.g. VAT

Direct tax - tax on income e.g. income tax

Specific/unit tax - fixed rate tax e.g. £1 per bottle of wine

Ad valorem tax - a % tax e.g. 15% on a bottle of wine so more tax is paid for a more expensive bottle.

Subsidy - money paid to producers to encourage production, often for goods with positive externalities e.g. sports centres.

State provision - government providing certain goods and services e.g. education.

Regulation - rules set by the government e.g. no smoking in public places

Information provision - government providing information to influence consumption e.g. encouraging people to have the covid vaccine.

Policies to Correct Externalities

Taxation

A tax is often used to reduce consumption of goods with negative externalities e.g. smoking.

- A tax increases the cost of production shifting the supply curve from S1 to S2.

- Price increases from P1 to P2.

- Quantity falls from Q1 to Q2 which corrects the market failure of overconsumption.

- The amount of tax paid by the consumer is the top rectangle.

- The amount of tax paid by the producer is the bottom rectangle.

- When demand is inelastic there is a small reduction in quantity so the tax is not as effective.

- When demand is inelastic a larger proportion of the tax is paid by the consumer.

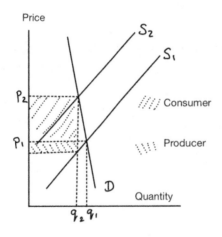
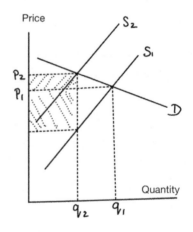

Advantages of Taxation

1. Consumption is reduced so the negative externality is reduced.

2. Those responsible for the negative externality are paying for it - the externality is internalised.

3. Government gets tax revenue which they can use to pay debt or spend on providing information to persuade smokers to reduce consumption, thus reducing the externality.

Disadvantages of Taxation

1. Ineffective if demand is inelastic.

2. Placing a monetary value on the externality is difficult.

3. The tax may be regressive so impact lower income consumers more

4. Cost of production is increased for firms so they become less internationally competitive which could lead to firms closing down and unemployment.

5. Firms may relocate abroad to avoid the tax.

6. The money received might not be used to correct the externality.

Subsidy

Used to encourage the consumption e.g. swimming pools

- A subsidy decreases the cost of production shifting S1 to S2.

- Price falls from P1 to P2.

- Quantity increases from q1 to q2 which corrects the market failure of underconsumption.

- The gain from the subsidy by the producer is the top rectangle.

- The gain from the subsidy by the consumer is the bottom rectangle.

- When demand is inelastic there is a small increase in quantity so the subsidy is not as effective.

- When demand is inelastic a larger proportion of the subsidy goes to the producer.

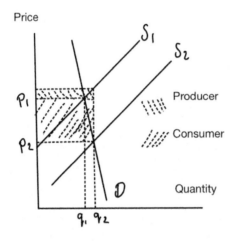
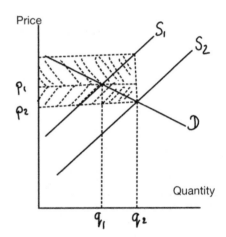

Advantages of Subsidies
- Increased consumption of goods with positive externalities.
- Price of the good falls.
- Subsidies can help infant industries until they are established enough to survive.
- Job creation in the subsidised market

Disadvantages of subsidies

- There will be an opportunity cost - the money could have been spent on something else.

- It is difficult to place a monetary value on the positive externalities so the market failure might not be fully corrected.

- Producers may rely on subsidies and have no incentive to be more efficient.

- If PED is inelastic the quantity will not increase by very much.

State Provision

- Governments use taxes to provide goods and services free of charge.

- These tend to be merit goods such as education and NHS or public goods which would otherwise not be provided e.g. street lights.

- The aim is to reduce the market failure of underconsumption.

Advantages of State Provision.

- Reduces inequality as everyone has access to the goods.

- Reduces market failure of underconsumption.

- Redistributes income as tax is used to pay for the goods.

- Healthier and better educated population.

Disadvantages of State Provision.

- Higher taxes required to pay for state provision.

- People who can afford to pay for themselves get the goods free of charge.

- Less incentive for these goods to be provided efficiently as no profit motive for the government.

- Deciding how much to provide is difficult eg too much then it is overconsumed/ wasted, too little there will be long waiting lists.

Regulations

These are used in many situations often to correct market failure and to protect consumers. Examples of regulation are

- Compulsory face masks indoors.

- Banning smoking in public places.

- Age restrictions on buying alcohol.

- Compulsory child booster seats.

- Energy companies must use a certain percentage of renewable energy.

- Workers maximum working weak and minimum required breaks.

Advantages of Regulation

- Encourages consumption of merit goods.

- Discourages the use of demerit goods.

- Encourages use of green energy.

- Safer working conditions.

- Protection of human rights.

- Higher standards.

Disadvantages of Regulation

- Often needs policing which costs.

- Difficult to get the level correct / appropriate.

- Can be expensive for firms to meet the regulations so prices may rise or they may go out of business.

- Could encourage a black market e.g. people illegally selling cigarettes.

Information Provision

- Giving consumers more information enables them to make an informed and rational choice about consumption.

- Reduces the asymmetric information e.g. compulsory food labelling allows consumers to see the sugar and fat content of foods before buying, this may encourage them to make different / better choices.

- Information provision will impact the demand for a product. E.g. providing information on the benefits of fruit and vegetables will shift demand to the right for fruit and vegetables. Providing information on the damaging effect of too much sugar will shift the demand curve for sugary products like chocolate to the left.

Advantages of Information Provision

- Can increase or decrease consumption by changing tastes and preferences of consumers

- Can be relatively cheap compared to subsidies

Disadvantages of Information Provision

- There may be a cost for firms or government - opportunity cost

- Consumers may ignore the information

Chapter 9. International Trade and the Global Economy

Definitions

International trade - exchanging goods and services between countries.

Imports - goods and services bought from other countries

Exports - goods and services sold abroad

Free trade area - no barriers to trade between countries within the area. Countries within the area impose their own barriers on other countries.

European Union (EU) - a group of European countries which have free trade between each other.

Balance of payments - a record of a countries transactions with the rest of the world.

Current account - trade in goods, services, income flows and transfers between one country and the rest of the world

Current account surplus – value of exports is greater than the value of imports.

Current account deficit – value of exports is less than the value of imports imports.

Exchange rate - the value of one currency in terms of another

Depreciation - fall in value of a floating exchange rate.

Appreciation - rise in the value of a floating exchange rate

Globalisation - increased integration between countries through more trade

Development - increasing living standards and quality of life

Developed country - a country with high GDP e.g. the UK

Less developed country - a country with low GDP e.g. Uganda

Importance of International Trade

Advantages of Specialisation and Trade
- Countries enjoy goods they are unable to produce due to the climate eg bananas and coffee cannot be produced in the UK.

- Larger variety of goods can be enjoyed not just the ones produced at home.

- Focusing on a small range of goods means countries can benefit from economies of scale to a greater extent.

- Countries focus on the goods and services which they are best at.

- Industries are able to grow and become more efficient.

Disadvantages of Specialisation and Trade
- High transport costs.

- Domestic industries will have more competition and may be forced out the market if they can't compete.

- If there are political conflicts trade is disrupted.

- If a country relies on another country for goods external factors such as Brexit or covid can make it difficult to get sufficient supply.

Free Trade Agreements
The European Union has free trade agreements with its members such as no tariffs (taxes) or quotas (limits on the amount that can be imported).

- Consumers can get cheaper goods from other countries
- Producers can sell abroad without a tariff on their good so the price will be lower abroad which increases demand
- Producers may have a higher output so can benefit from greater economies of scale
- Producers may find it hard to compete with the cheaper foreign goods
- Local firms may close if they can't compete which will lead to job losses

The Balance of Payments

Current Account
There are 4 sections:
1. Trade in goods eg clothes, cars

2. Trade in services eg employing a tutor based in another country, tourism.

3. Primary income - income from employment or investments eg dividends on shares in another country, profits from a company based abroad.

4. Secondary income - money moving between countries for which no work is done eg remittances (money sent home to family members when someone works abroad), foreign aid.

The UK usually has a large deficit on the current account.

Causes of a Deficit on the Current Account
- UK goods are more expensive than goods abroad eg due to higher labour costs.

- The quality of UK goods is worse than goods abroad.

- Inflation is higher in the UK than other countries.

- An increase in the exchange rate causes UK goods to be more expensive abroad.

-

Problems with a Current Account Deficit
- There will be lower demand for UK goods which could lead to lower growth and loss of jobs.

- Less demand for UK goods means less demand for pounds. This will lead to a fall in the exchange rate. Imported raw material become more expensive. This could lead to cost push inflation.

- The deficit needs to be funded by borrowing on the capital account. The borrowed money needs to be paid back with interest.

- A deficit may suggest a country is uncompetitive.

When is a Deficit not a Problem-

- If it is small in comparison to national income.

- If it is for a short period of time.

Policies to Correct Imbalances on the Current Account

These can be split into two categories

1. **Expenditure switching policies** - aim to switch spending from foreign goods to home produced goods.

- Restrictions on imports e.g. tariffs and quotas

- Subsidies to home firms to help them lower costs of production.

- Depreciate the exchange rate to make home produced goods cheaper abroad.

- Supply-side policies to encourage efficiency and reduce costs of production.

2. **Expenditure reducing policies** - aimed at reducing spending which will reduce spending on home produced goods as well as imports.

- Tight fiscal policy e.g. increasing income tax so consumers have less disposable income.

- Tight monetary policy e.g. increasing interest rates so consumers are less likely to spend.

Exchange Rates

Changes in the Value of an Exchange Rate

Anything which causes the supply or demand for a currency to change will have an impact on the exchange rate. There will be an increase in the demand for pounds from D1 to D2 which increases the exchange rate.

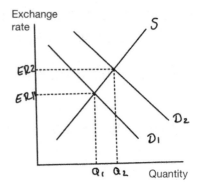

- Incomes abroad increase so more demand for UK goods. Pounds are needed to buy UK goods.

- Quality of UK goods improves so more demand for UK goods.

- Interest rates in the UK increase. The flow of hot money into the UK to put into UK banks will increase.

- Inflation in the UK is lower than other countries so increased demand for UK goods.

- A major sporting event in the UK will increase the number of tourists who will need pounds.

- Expectation that the value of the pound will increase. Speculators will buy pounds in order to sell when the value increases further.

- Government increases the demand for pounds (they sell foreign reserves).

If there is an increase in supply of pounds there will be a decrease in the exchange rate.

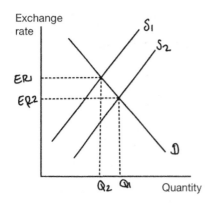

- UK incomes increase so more demand for imports. Pounds are supplied in exchange for foreign currency which is needed to buy the imports.

- Quality of foreign goods improves so more demand for foreign goods. Supply of pounds increases in exchange for the foreign currency.

- Interest rates in the UK fall. Hot money will leave the UK in search of higher interest rates, elsewhere.

- Inflation in the UK is higher than other countries so there will be more demand for imports. Foreign currency is needed to buy the imports.

- A major sporting event abroad so pounds are exchanged in exchange for foreign currency.

- Speculators expect the value of the pound will fall so want to sell before it falls too low.

- Government supplies pounds from their reserves and demands foreign currency.

Impacts on the Economy
A fall in the value of the pound will have the following impact:
- Exports become cheaper so demand will increase.

- Imports become more expensive so demand will fall.

- Net exports will increase.

- The current account of the balance of payments will improve.

- More demand for UK goods will increase aggregate demand.

- Economic growth will increase.

- Labour is a derived demand so unemployment will fall.

- Inflation may increase.

Impact on Consumers (of a fall in the ER)
- Imports become more expensive

- Lower standard of living due to imports being more expensive

- More expensive to go on holiday abroad

- Inflation may increase due to increased price of imports

Impact on Producers (of a fall in the ER)

- UK goods are cheaper abroad so more exports

- UK consumers more likely to buy UK goods due to imports being more expensive

- Tourism to the UK will be cheaper

- Raw materials which are imported will be more expensive so costs of production increase which means prices may increase.

Globalisation

Driving Factors of Globalisation

- Reduction of barriers

This makes trade easier and cheaper. Countries can get access to cheaper raw materials and technology which enables them to grow.

- . Improvement in transport

Better transport links makes it easier to transport raw materials and finished goods. Investment in transport infrastructure has been vital.

- .Foreign Investment

The growth of MNCs such as Nike and Apple has increased growth and investment in other countries.

- Advances in technology

The internet has enabled more trade to take place. Communication over trade in goods is easier and there is more trade in services eg online tutoring.

Measures of Development

- GDP per capita

- Life expectancy

- Access to healthcare

- Technology e.g. % of population with mobile phones

- Education e.g. literacy rate or mean years of schooling

Costs and Benefits of Globalisation

Developed Countries

Producers

- May go out of business if foreign firms are cheaper

- Increased admin costs of trading overseas

- If incomes aboard fall there could be a large impact in terms of lower demand

- Wider marker to sell goods to

- Cheaper raw materials

- Wider choice of raw materials

- Access to more skilled labour from other countries

- Access to cheaper labour from other countries

Workers

- If industries decline eg manufacturing in the UK there will be loss of jobs

- Increased use of technology means job losses or the need to learn new skills

- Increased immigration means more competition for jobs

- Greater output could mean more workers employed

- Increased foreign investment could lead to more jobs

- Ability to move to other countries for work

Consumers

- Possible increased prices due to more consumers competing for the goods

- Less choice if global brands push local firms out of business

- More fluctuations on prices if exchange rates are fluctuating

- Wider range of goods due to more imports

- Lower prices due to increased competition

- Better quality goods and services

- More opportunities for travel

Economic, Social and Environmental Sustainability

Economic - less efficient industries will suffer as they cannot compete. In the longer term economies will adjust so the developed countries will likely focus more on services.

Social - greater choice and lower priced goods improves standards of living. However, there will be increased unemployment in certain industries.

Environmental - countries specialise in the goods they are best at but there will be increased pollution from transporting good.

Less Developed Countries

Producers

- External shocks leaves producers vulnerable e.g. bad weather means they may not have as much of their crops to export

- Skilled workers may move abroad where they get paid more

- Smaller countries may not be able to compete so firms go out of business

- Wider market to sell goods to

- Access to better technology

- Increased investment from abroad

Workers

- Machines may replace workers

- If demand for exports falls due to the country being less efficient, there will be job losses

- Greater gap between rich and poor, owners of the businesses are better off.

- Poor working conditions due to less regulation - developed countries often exploit the workers

- Increased job opportunities

- Ability to work in other countries where pay is better

Consumers

- Higher prices as more consumers competing to buy the goods

- Possibly poor quality services e.g. teachers due to workers moving abroad

- Wider range of goods

- Access to global brands eg Nike and Apple

- Greater opportunity for travel

- Better infrastructure due to foreign investment

Economic, Social and Environmental Sustainability

Economic - greater tax revenue due to increased trade, more employment likely and higher economic growth. However, if MNCs leave this will not last.

Social - increased income due to increased employment, poverty will be lower. However, cultural diversity may be lost and prices may increase.

Environmental - countries specialise in what they are best at so produce more efficiently. However, transporting the raw materials and goods lead to increased pollution.

Notes

Notes

Notes

Notes

Notes

Notes

Notes

Notes

Notes

Notes

This revision guide is based on the OCR GCSE specification.

The aim is to provide you with summary notes and key terms on all of the topics.

Specification links are given in the contents

Printed in Great Britain
by Amazon

39065585R00046